Joyful
Thankful
Prayerful

a journal that organizes
your prayer time

Courtney Sikes Moore

All Things Beautiful Letters Publishing
Fort Worth, Texas

All Things Beautiful Letters Publishing
PO Box 12602
Fort Worth, Texas 76110

ISBN: 10: 1983513881
ISBN-13: 978-1983513886

May God use this book to bless your prayer time + grow your God dreams!

Love,
Courtney

DEDICATION

This prayer journal is dedicated to my mother, Patricia Thomasson Sikes, who loves me unconditionally, always points me back to Jesus and has prayed all the hard prayers over my life and my walk with Jesus.

CONTENTS

INTRODUCTION

If you're anything like me, you know in your heart that your prayer life is the pulse of your relationship with God. But, that consistently keeping that daily meeting with Him is one of our biggest struggles. We value our time and our sleep over everything the Lord wants to share with us.

And every missed opportunity to meet with Him is a delay on some amazing things He's planned to whisper into your heart. It's procrastinating on getting to know the One who knows you better than anyone else.

My dear friend Whitney and I had to the opportunity to attend a relatively small Beth Moore conference in 2017 called Lit. One of the things Beth told us as she broke down her writing process for us was that seventy percent of what she writes comes directly from prayer time.

And I don't want to miss anything that God has planned for me. I don't want to miss knowing more about the One who loves me more than anyone else is capable of.

In 1 Thessalonians 5:16-18, we are called to always be joyful, to pray every opportunity we get and to be thankful no matter what the situation is. The Passion Translation even says to make your life a prayer. I don't know how else we can have that much joy and gratitude and to pray unceasingly unless we have regular prayer time, keep a prayer journal and ask God to keep that daily date with Him.

I'm praying that we would all become more joyful, more thankful and more prayerful. Not because we are that capable of it, but because of what we are letting Him and asking Him to accomplish in us and through us.

I can't wait to hear how God is using your prayer time with Him to do BIG things!

#joyfulthankfulprayerfulprayerjournal

love,
Courtney

This is where you start. The purpose of this page is to tune your heart to God's heart. List out all the ways you can possibly praise and thank God today for who He is, what He has done, what He is doing and what He's about to do!

tune my heart to sing your praise

date _____

_____
_____
_____
_____
_____
_____

thank you, Lord...

_____
_____
_____
_____
_____

atb.

And here's the place where you keeping knocking on that door. You've just listed out all the ways you're praising God and all the ways you're thanking Him. By the time you get to this page, whatever seemed so giant will seem pretty small compared to our big and capable God. And there is also an answered prayers section so you can make notes of those awesome moments, look back over God's goodness and even see how He changes our will to fit His Will!

pray persistently

answered prayer

alb.

This is where you are going to let God lead you in the places where He's called you. This is where His truths and direction will pour out and where you can journal the ways God is speaking to your heart during your prayer time. There is a scripture section where you can reference the verses you happen to be camping on. Pray with your Bible open and let God equip you.

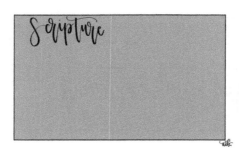

Every seventh day you will get a page like this. It is also meant to enrich your prayer life. Your pastor may lay a word on your heart that God means to carry you that week. You need to be in prayer about it, this allows you to capture those moments.

date **Sermon Notes**

_____

_____

_____

_____

_____

_____

_____ **Scripture**

_____

_____

_____

god speaking to me _____

_____

_____ *atb.*

The Journal

Courtney Sikes Moore

*tune my heart
to sing Your praise*

date

_____

_____

_____

_____

_____

thank You, Lord...

_____

_____

_____

_____

_____

alb.

pray persistently

answered prayer

date

Layed on my heart

Scripture

Courtney Sikes Moore

tune my heart to sing Your praise

date

thank You, Lord...

atb.

pray persistently

answered prayer

date

Layed on my heart

Scripture

Courtney Sikes Moore

tune my heart to sing Your praise

date

thank You, Lord...

aLb.

pray persistently

answered prayer

date

Layed on my heart

Scripture

Courtney Sikes Moore

date

tune my heart to sing Your praise

_____

_____

_____

_____

_____

thank You, Lord...

_____

_____

_____

_____

_____

atb.

pray persistently

answered prayer

date

Scripture

Courtney Sikes Moore

date

tune my heart
to sing your praise

_____

_____

_____

_____

_____

_____

thank You, Lord...

_____

_____

_____

_____

_____

atb.

pray persistently

answered prayer

date

Layed on my heart

Scripture

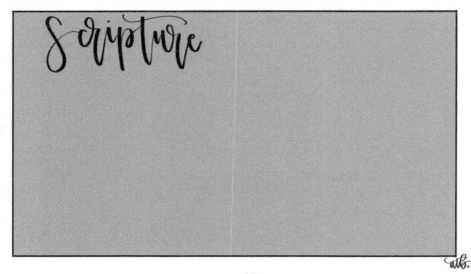

tune my heart to sing Your praise

date

_____

_____

_____

_____

_____

_____

thank You, Lord...

_____

_____

_____

_____

_____

atb.

pray persistently

answered prayer

_____

_____

_____

_____

_____

_____

_____

_____

_____

_____

_____

_____

_____

_____

_____

alb.

date

Layed on my heart

Scripture

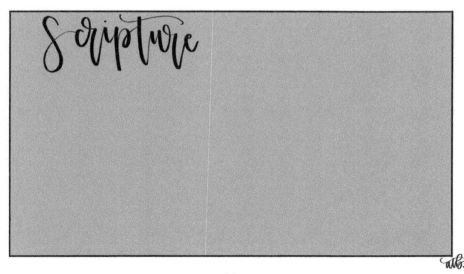

Courtney Sikes Moore

*tune my heart
to sing Your praise*

date

_____

_____

_____

_____

_____

_____

thank You, Lord...

_____

_____

_____

_____

_____

_____

alb.

pray persistently

answered prayer

date

Layed on my heart

Scripture

Sermon Notes

_____

_____

_____

_____

_____

_____

_____ scripture

_____

_____

_____

_____

god speaking to me _____

_____

_____

_____

atb.

*tune my heart
to sing Your praise*

date

_____

_____

_____

_____

_____

_____

thank You, Lord...

_____

_____

_____

_____

_____

_____

atb.

pray persistently

answered prayer

date

Layed on my heart

Scripture

Courtney Sikes Moore

*tune my heart
to sing Your praise*

date

thank You, Lord...

atb.

pray persistently

answered prayer

date

Layed on my heart

Scripture

date

tune my heart to sing your praise

_____

_____

_____

_____

_____

thank you, Lord...

_____

_____

_____

_____

_____

atb.

pray persistently

answered prayer

date

Layed on my heart

Scripture

Courtney Sikes Moore

tune my heart to sing Your praise

date

_____

_____

_____

_____

_____

thank You, Lord...

_____

_____

_____

_____

_____

pray persistently

answered prayer

date

Layed on my heart

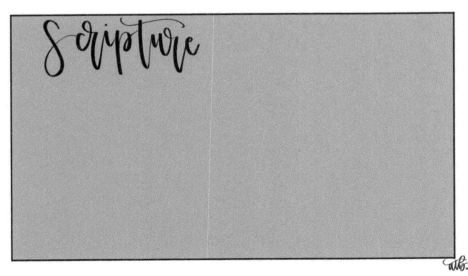

Scripture

tune my heart
to sing Your praise

date

thank You, Lord...

alb.

pray persistently

answered prayer

date

Layed on my heart

Scripture

Courtney Sikes Moore

tune my heart to sing your praise

date

thank you, Lord...

aVb.

pray persistently

answered prayer

_____

_____

_____

_____

_____

_____

_____

_____

_____

_____

_____

_____

_____

_____

date

Layed on my heart

Scripture

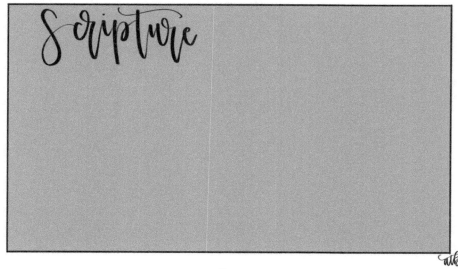

Courtney Sikes Moore

date

tune my heart to sing your praise

_____

_____

_____

_____

_____

thank you, Lord...

_____

_____

_____

_____

_____

_____

atb.

pray persistently

answered prayer

_____

_____

_____

_____

_____

_____

_____

_____

_____

_____

_____

_____

_____

_____

_____

_____

alb.

date

Layed on my heart

Scripture

date

Sermon Notes

scripture

god speaking to me

date

tune my heart to sing Your praise

_____

_____

_____

_____

_____

_____

thank You, Lord...

_____

_____

_____

_____

_____

_____

alb.

pray persistently

answered prayer

date

Layed on my heart

Scripture

Courtney Sikes Moore

date

tune my heart
to sing Your praise

---

thank You, Lord...

---

aNB.

pray persistently

answered prayer

date

Layed on my heart

Scripture

Courtney Sikes Moore

tune my heart to sing Your praise

date

_____

_____

_____

_____

_____

_____

thank You, Lord...

_____

_____

_____

_____

_____

alb.

pray persistently

answered prayer

date

Layed on my heart

Scripture

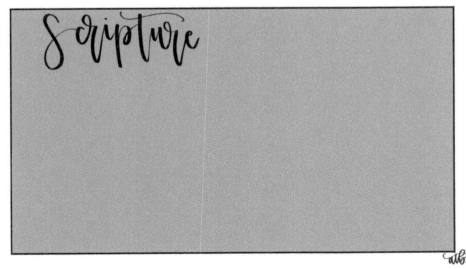

*tune my heart
to sing your praise*

date

_____

_____

_____

_____

_____

thank you, Lord...

_____

_____

_____

_____

_____

atb.

pray persistently

answered prayer

date

Layed on my heart

Scripture

tune my heart to sing Your praise

date

_____

_____

_____

_____

_____

thank You, Lord...

_____

_____

_____

_____

_____

_____

atb.

pray persistently

answered prayer

date

Layed on my heart

Scripture

Courtney Sikes Moore

date

tune my heart to sing your praise

_____

_____

_____

_____

_____

thank you, Lord...

_____

_____

_____

_____

_____

alb.

pray persistently

answered prayer

date

Layed on my heart

Scripture

Courtney Sikes Moore

date

tune my heart
to sing Your praise

_____

_____

_____

_____

_____

_____

thank You, Lord...

_____

_____

_____

_____

_____

atb.

pray persistently

answered prayer

date

Layed on my heart

Scripture

date

Sermon Notes

Scripture

god speaking to me

tune my heart to sing your praise

date

_____

_____

_____

_____

_____

_____

thank You, Lord...

_____

_____

_____

_____

_____

_____

atb.

pray persistently

answered prayer

date

Layed on my heart

Scripture

Courtney Sikes Moore

tune my heart
to sing Your praise

date

_____

_____

_____

_____

_____

thank You, Lord...

_____

_____

_____

_____

_____

alb.

pray persistently

answered prayer

date

Layed on my heart

Scripture

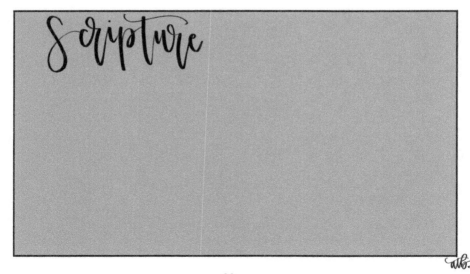

Courtney Sikes Moore

tune my heart to sing your praise

date

thank you, Lord...

atb.

pray persistently

answered prayer

date

Layed on my heart

Scripture

Courtney Sikes Moore

tune my heart to sing your praise

date _____

_____

_____

_____

_____

_____

_____

thank you, Lord...

_____

_____

_____

_____

_____

atb.

pray persistently

answered prayer

date

Layed on my heart

Scripture

Courtney Sikes Moore

date

tune my heart
to sing your praise

_____

_____

_____

_____

_____

thank you, Lord...

_____

_____

_____

_____

_____

atB.

pray persistently

answered prayer

date

Layed on my heart

Scripture

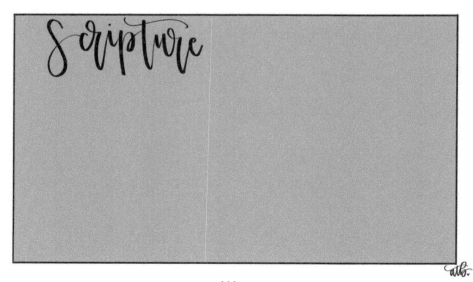

Courtney Sikes Moore

tune my heart to sing your praise

date

thank you, Lord...

atb.

pray persistently

answered prayer

date

Layed on my heart

Scripture

Courtney Sikes Moore

date

tune my heart to sing Your praise

_____

_____

_____

_____

_____

thank You, Lord...

_____

_____

_____

_____

_____

_____

atb.

pray persistently

answered prayer

date

Layed on my heart

Scripture

date

Sermon Notes

scripture

god speaking to me

tune my heart to sing your praise

date _____

_____

_____

_____

_____

_____

thank you, Lord...

_____

_____

_____

_____

_____

atb.

pray persistently

answered prayer

Joyful Thankful Prayerful

date

Layed on my heart

Scripture

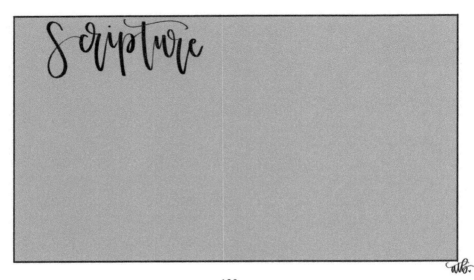

123

Courtney Sikes Moore

tune my heart to sing Your praise

date

---

thank You, Lord...

atb.

pray persistently

answered prayer

date

Layed on my heart

Scripture

Courtney Sikes Moore

ACKNOWLEDGEMENTS

All of the glory for this prayer journal goes to Jesus. Thank you for saving my life, showing me how to pray + loving me fiercely. Thank you God for being in complete control of my life + for all the plans you've made for me. Thank you Holy Spirit for equipping me for what God has called me to do, for every teaching moment + every reminder.

Thank you to my husband, Aaron, for all your love, encouragement + support. He loved the idea of this prayer journal from the beginning + cheered me on. Thank you to our daughter, Stevie, for always giving me plenty of prayer material. Thank you to Bible Study Fellowship International for training me to teach God's Word + being the place where I learned to pray bold prayers, praise God even in the struggle + call on His name. Thank you to my Arborlawn United Methodist Church family. Your love + encouragement is life giving.

Thank you to my spiritual mothers for consistently loving me + pointing me to Jesus

Thank you to Karen Anderson for helping me put this book together. Without her I would be hand-lettering them one by one. Thank you for praying with me + keeping me accountable, precious friend!

Thank you to Whitney Scott for being my amazingly encouraging sister in the faith, for praying 1 Thessalonians 5:16-18 with me every day for 30 days + for how willing you are to go on all the Jesus adventures with me!

Thank you to my family for the Jesus culture that lives + breathes in every one of our family gatherings. We have the best talks! And thank you to my mom + dad for the way they pray. Together, out loud + in front of us. It's important. We see you. Our children see you. Please keep planting Jesus.

ABOUT THE AUTHOR

Courtney Sikes Moore is a hand-lettering artist from Fort Worth, Texas where she resides with her husband and daughter. She developed her hand-lettering business, All Things Beautiful Letters, based on Ecclesiastes 3:11 which says that all things are made beautiful according to God's timing. Through All Things Beautiful, she focuses on God's calling to hand-letter His Word, His truths and His promises. She feels that God has called her to hand-letter His Word as beautifully as it speaks to her heart.

Instagram: @allthingsbeautifulletters
Facebook: @abtletters
Twitter: @csmooremerrier
Etsy: www.etsy.com/shop/ATBLetters

Courtney Sikes Moore